A **Struggle** for God

A Study Guide

Canyon, Texas
Carpediempublishers.com

Copyright © 2017 Jessica Smith
All rights reserved. No part of this book may be
reproduced in any form without the written permission of
the Author or Carpe Diem Publishers.

ISBN 978-0-9836691-1-1

A Struggle for God

A Study Guide

Jessica Smith
with

Jay Loyd and Rebecca Woody

Edited by: Annie Preston, LLC

First readers/original editors:

Jay Loyd
Rebecca Woody
Kyle Smith

Final editor:

Annie Preston, LLC

Cover
Photo: Jessica Smith
Design: Rory C. Keel

What's in the Book?

Part One
　　　Story..2

Part Two
　　　Monologue...20

Part Three
　　　Study Guide Questions..28
　　　Answers/Opinions..36

To my sweet son, Nathan-

My deepest hope is for you to decide to love God with all your heart. I hope you choose to be a strong, Christian man and a humble servant to God all the days of your life. I urge you to choose a loving, Christian wife who will help you raise your children the same. I look forward to sharing an eternity in Heaven with you and all those in God's Kingdom. I am so proud of you.

Love,
Mom

Part One

THE STORY:

Joseph Welling picked up the can of sky blue paint and poured the rest of it into the paint trough. He rolled on another thick layer of the peaceful hue and finished the fourth wall in the game room. The boys were still outside. It was a beautiful day with typical late June weather, a warm 93 degrees and sunny. The grass was green and growing, and the flowers were in full bloom. The older boys had been mowing the two-and-a-half-acres while the younger boys were picking up trash and weeds. They took pride in their home; it was after all a safe place to live and most certainly peaceful, which is something many of them hadn't ever known before they ended up here.

Joseph and his wife, Elle, maintain a loving foster home for nine boys ranging in age from six to seventeen. They mean the world to Joseph and Elle.

Mikey (6), is the youngest and painfully shy.

James (8), is the adventurous one.

Bradly (12), is a reader and quiet as a mouse.

Joshua (12), is talkative and excited about everything.

Danny (14), is the creative type and likes to build things.

Matty (15), is an amazing kid; he is autistic and is a brilliant piano player.

Trent (16), wants to be knowledgeable and is interested in all the finer points of how things work.

Hayden (17), is outspoken, loves cars and things that go fast.

Zeke (17), is a gentle giant, his brothers' keeper, and a rule follower.

The boys all have different stories, some bad and some really bad. Four of them (Bradly, Danny, Trent, and Hayden) had parents that loved being high more than they could ever love a child, even their own. The State took these boys from their parents. Joshua, Matty, and Zeke had parents that didn't believe they were ready for children or didn't think they could handle the stress that came with parenting---whatever their reasons----they gave their children away. Two brothers (Mikey and James) lost their parents in a boating accident. Those poor little boys had no family left and no godmother or godfather in line to take on the responsibility of raising them. Their parents were English but lived in America before their deaths.

Joseph and Elle have been keeping abandoned boys for twenty-two years now---since 1966. They live in Monroeville, Alabama, which is made up of the wonderfully plush green landscape, rich blue skies, and big bulky trees. Their farm is filled with trees that are perfect for young boys to climb. Both Joseph and his wife are in their mid-fifties, with much wisdom and an exceptional amount of love for these boys. They are all but licensed counselors, ministers, and physicians. Every single boy that comes through their home, they love as their own.

Dishes have to be done twice a day and vacuuming, every two days. Laundry---let's not even go there. Even with all the work of keeping, loving and raising nine boys, it is well worth the reward, and the boys grow up thinking of Joseph and Elle as their own parents. They refer to them as mom and dad, and though all nine of them had something terrible in their past that separated them from their biological parents, they have all been with the Wellings long enough to create new memories to overshadow the dark ones. The boys become brothers, too. When new boys come into the foster home, they are naturally distant at first, but soon come to join in and form strong bonds with their new brothers. When they become adults and leave, it's just like any family sending off a sibling to college. There is something amazing about a young person coming from vulnerability that makes them cling so strongly to love and sustainability when they find it.

Joseph had just finished painting the room when Jackson came running up to him and pounced on his chest. Jackson is a loyal friend and extremely close to Joseph. He hugged Joseph with all nineteen pounds of his furry body. Jackson is a full-blooded mutt. He has a little of everything in him. He has the traits of the wise, smart dogs, the calm dogs, the adventurous dogs, the playful, loving dogs, the protective dogs, and of course, the loyal dogs. He looks like he is mostly foxhound with maybe some collie in him. No one is sure, but they are sure of his place in the family. Everybody loves Jackson. He sleeps in a different boy's room each night, making his rounds through the week. But he is closest to Joseph. They do everything together and go everywhere together. Jackson is pretty well known in Monroeville. As Joseph calls to Jackson, "Let's go!" he heads to the truck and jumps up into his seat. Sitting on his rubber mat in the truck makes him feel like a king. Joseph heads to the store to pick up food for dinner that night and picks up a little snack for Jackson like he does every time they go to the store. Same snack as always: a can of black olives. This dog loves olives. He will do just about anything for an olive. He likes them room-temperature. When they get back to the house, Joseph opens the can of olives and pours them into Jackson's bowl. "Good boy."

As Joseph sits down in his big, brown recliner in the living room, he is inspecting the space, trying to decide how he is going to renovate it. Since he retired from being the fire chief in Monroeville, he has been renovating the house, room by room. Elle has always stayed home with the boys to look after them. He's wanted to renovate for a while, and now that he is retired, he can finally put more time into it. Twenty-two years of boys in their home has taken a toll on the house. They have had their share of things damaged, holes in the walls repaired, and light fixtures broken and replaced. Here is a fun fact: God made boys rowdy. The boys can see he is examining the room and pipe in with their own renovation ideas.

"I think we need a huge built-in TV right here, Dad!" announces Joshua. "And make this room green and blue, plus, let's put a dinner table right here so we can see the TV better when we're eating!"

"Yeah!" They all chimed in. Jackson jumped around in the middle of them.

"Do you think that's a good idea, Jackson?" Joseph asks in a high pitched goofy voice.

"Will we be destroying any walls in this room? Let's take out a wall!" suggests Hayden. Here is another fun fact: God gave boys an incredible love for absolute destruction.

Elle looks at Joseph and laughs. "It's so strange how getting them to separate their dirty laundry is like pulling teeth, but you ask them to obliterate a wall, and they come running like little worker ants with sledgehammers in hand."

Joseph laughs again, "I don't think we will be tearing down any walls this time boys, but we might change the color in here, move some things around, replace and repair a few things...sound good?"

"Yeah, that'll be good." offers Zeke.

From the moment each of the boys arrived there, Joseph worked to form a father-son relationship with each of them. Truth be known, sometimes he just makes up projects for all of them to do together, just so they can do father-son-and-brother things. They learn a lot from him. Every day, Joseph and Elle strive to teach each boy the value of hard work, respect for others, and above all, a love for God. They want their boys to have the best chance at having good lives.

"We will pick a couple of colors that go together and then start from there," says Joseph.

"Stay within the theme you guys!" yells Elle from the other room.

"Stay within the seam?" James asks Bradly.

"No, theme. Stay within the theme. Like the theme in a home," explains Bradly.

Young James nods and starts trying to figure out what movie they are trying to look like in the house. "Or maybe it is a theme from a book?" he thinks to himself.

Joseph tells the boys they will get started on the living room renovation as soon as they pick the colors. He tells them to grab their fishing poles in the meantime, and meet him at the pond.

They have a large, glassy pond about three hundred yards behind the house and the boys love fishing out there. Fishing with Dad is on the top of most of their lists of fun things to do. It is peaceful and green. It's a perfect summer thing to do while they aren't in school. That and going to the beach. They are fairly close to Florida and its soft, white sands, so they take regular trips to the beach as well. Another fun fact: The beach is a great place to take a bunch of boys with too much energy.

The boys race each other to the pond. Elle packs a snack bag for Joseph to take with him.

"We'll be back before dark," Joseph says to Elle.

She watches him leave with Jackson by his side. Jackson pushes on the creaky, screen door before Joseph gets there. He knows just how to push on it so he can get in and out without bothering anyone.

Joseph turns back to look at Elle and says, "These boys mean the world to me." Then he pats Jackson on the head and says to his wife in the most endearing way, "And this is my best friend." Joseph looks at Jackson and says, "Alright buddy! Let's go fishing with the boys!"

Elle yells out to them, "I put a can of olives in there for Jackson!"

A few days later, Joseph was ready to go into town to pick up the paint cans for the living room.

"Anyone want to go with me? Aside from you Jackson,

I know you want to go!" Joseph says, giving a short laugh. Danny, Trent, and Hayden jump up and run toward the truck.

"Okay, come on fellas, seatbelts on." Joseph gently orders.

Jackson is, of course, riding in his spot on the rubber mat. Once they get there, everyone hops out and heads toward the entrance of the home improvement store. On their way in, the boys notice a big banner strung tightly across two posts and pushed into the plush green lawn. The sign across the street read: Smithsonian Museum Here Today! They tell Joseph that they are going over there to check it out and will be right in.

Joseph nods that it is fine for them to check it out. "Watch for cars, boys!"

They head to the mall across the street to see what the Smithsonian banner is all about. Many people are coming and going from the east section of the mall.

"It must be over there!" Danny announces.

They see a few men in nice blazer jackets standing in front of another museum banner. "They must be with the four big, black charter buses and the nice looking, shiny black car out front, what do you wanna bet?" says Hayden.

They move closer to look at what the men are selling.

"I have heard of this museum before, but I don't know much about it," says Trent.

The first thing they see is a really small, angry-looking dog, yapping like crazy.

"These men don't look like they are from around here, and neither does that small dog," says Hayden.

"Looks like they are selling really expensive watches and

jewelry. Hey, we should get something for mom and dad," suggests Danny. "It is mom's birthday in five days and dad's in twenty-four!"

"Really Danny?" Trent questions, rolling his eyes. "Number one, I can't believe you know the exact number of days until their birthdays and number two, we didn't bring any money with us."

Then Trent and Hayden look at each other. Danny notices them making a weird eye contact.

"What are you guys doing?" probes Danny.

"Nothing, we're thinking," Trent answers.

"Thinking what?" pushes Danny.

Hayden adds his two cents. "These people clearly have lots of money. I am sure they won't even notice if we take one thing for Mom and one thing for Dad."

"Really?!" asks Danny.

"Yes, definitely! They're loaded. They will never notice," defends Trent.

Hayden grabs Danny and tells him that he and Trent need his help. They tell him to distract the men in the nice blue blazers while they pick out two cool things, one for Mom and one for Dad. Danny hesitates a little, but seeing his older brothers look enthusiastically at him; he agrees to help.

"Okay, I will stall them with a lot of long questions that will take a long time to answer!"

"Good Danny, that will work!" says Trent. Hayden nods in agreement.

Trent and Hayden stay close together while they look over the items on display. They quietly slide the glass casing door slowly to the left and pick the two items they want. While they are trying to put them in their pockets, the yappy, little dog starts barking in that annoying high-pitched voice. It startles both of them, and they start moving away from the fancy, marble tables. The dog quickly jumps out of the chair it was in and hastily starts running after the two boys. They bolt through the first door to their right, and the dog follows after them. The street is almost immediately behind the back entrance to the mall, so they quickly turn. The dog follows after them and stumbles into the street.

Then tragedy strikes. Without warning, a car rushes by and hits the little dog. He is killed instantly. Trent and Hayden stop to look at each other. The men in the nice blue blazers are running out the same door to catch up to them. One of them runs up to where the dog is lying in the street. He kneels down next to him. His face is showing signs of pain; then tears start rolling down his cheeks.

"Oh no, no, no, no. My little Chihuahua!"

He looks at the boys and yells, "What happened?!"

Without giving them time to respond, he sees the two very expensive pieces of jewelry the boys stole, and exclaims, "Did you take those items?! Do you know what that is or how expensive those two relics are? We are from the Smithsonian! We are traveling to showcase and promote the museum! Very few can afford these relics. They are over eight hundred thousand dollars apiece!" he scolded. Then he looked down again at his dog.

"My little dog, oh no, no, no."

Trent and Hayden lay the relics down by his side while the blue blazer man knelt next to his dog.

Joseph finally makes his way over to the mall side of the street and is about to head in to get the boys, when he sees Trent standing over by the east side of the mall. He turns and clicks the lock button on his key fob and the truck honks as its alarm system is activated.

"I'll be right back," he tells Jackson, who is in the back of the truck. Joseph looks back at Trent and scrunches his nose in confusion, not knowing why Trent would be way over there. He gets closer and sees the other two boys near an older man.

"What's going on here?" he asks in a very concerned way. The boys can tell he's not mad, but he is definitely concerned.

The man's face turns fire truck red.

With a heavy Italian accent, he belts out, "My precious little dog is dead because your two boys tried to steal these highly expensive, historic relics from our museum collection!"

"Oh, my..." Joseph answered. He looked over at the boys, concerned and confused.

"I am so sorry about your dog sir. What can I do? Is there anything I can do? Is there some way I can repay you?" Joseph was very apologetic.

The man glared at Joseph and the two boys and not expecting an answer, he asked, "Do you know what 18 U.S. Code § 668-Theft of major artwork says? It says prison up to 10 years for theft of museum property along with a steep fine! The museum has its own lawyers, but this will be charged by the State! All we need to do is charge your boys. Trust me! We will!" He said with spit flying from his mouth.

"Your oldest here will be charged as an adult! You can count on it!"

Fear overcame Hayden.

"Oh, sir please, please don't charge them," asks Joseph. "I can pay you."

"You can't afford these relics. They are over eight hundred thousand dollars apiece," says the man.

"Oh, my..." Joseph turned pale. He looks at the two boys and sees that they are very scared. He begs the man, "Please don't charge them. Please, sir, take the relics back. They are unharmed."

The man looks back at Joseph then over to his truck and sees a curious dog sitting in the back like a prince. With anger and spite in his heart, he says, "You can give me your dog. My dog is dead, you can give me yours, and we will not press charges against your boys."

Joseph's stomach was in his throat. "He is my best friend. My loyal companion. I love him. How can you put me in such a situation?"

"That is my offer," the man responded.

Joseph slowly walked back to his truck, feeling completely defeated. He pulled the truck bed down and sat beside his companion and talked quietly with him for a good while. As full tears streamed down his face, he began to reminisce when he brought Jackson home for the first time. His tail, uncontrollably wagging back and forth. He remembered well the first ride to the house, and the first time Elle met Jackson. Those memories were priceless. He recalled the first time he realized the dog's love for black olives. He chuckled a tearful laugh as he thought about Jackson sneaking up to the table where Elle had put out a saucer full of black olives for the boys to put in their side salads that night for dinner. Needless to say, none of the boys had olives in their salads that night. He remembered fishing at the pond on their land, and once fishing was over, giving the "Go ahead" to Jackson that it was okay to jump in the water. He is a natural swimmer.

Jackson had been in their lives long enough that Joseph felt that sometimes he could almost say exactly what Jackson was thinking. A loyal companion he is. He held Jackson tightly and cried as hard as he could, hoping to bring some relief to himself by the outflow of emotion that overcame his heart. He wished Jackson had been taking a nap or on an adventure outside when he left the house earlier. If only he hadn't been with us this time. He ached with regret for eagerly asking Jackson to come along. He battled back and forth over whether he should allow his sons to pay for their mistakes and let the outcome be as it will. He considered his chances of getting an attorney to help his side of the case and considered whether he would even have the funds for that.

Joseph had a choice. He was either going to allow his sons to pay the cost with a high chance of going to prison, at least for Hayden, or give up his loyal companion, Jackson. His heart ached as it never had before. His nausea moved up his stomach and he leaned over the side of the truck. He couldn't hold it back.

He whispered to Jackson, "It was never your fault. It is not you. No part of me wants this." Jackson licked his face. He hoped somehow Jackson would understand how much his heart was broken that he had to give Jackson to the man with the Italian accent.

Holding his dog tightly in his arms, Joseph walked back toward the man. His nose was running, and his eyes were soaked with tears. He put Jackson in the other man's vehicle and told his boys to go to the truck. Jackson gave a little whine and cocked his head to the right like he always did when he wasn't sure what was going on.

Joseph turned back around and looked at him straight in the eyes and said, "I will always love you, my Jackson. You are my best friend." With heavy sadness, Joseph turned his head back toward the boys and couldn't look back again. His stomach turned with nausea again, and new tears welled up in his eyes.

With everyone in the truck, Joseph turned on the ignition; you could hear a pin drop. He sat still for a few minutes feeling the truck rattle beneath him. His hands and feet felt numb. His eyes stayed fixed on the dash, only blinking to release the flow of saline every few seconds. The boys were nervous, not knowing what was coming next.

Joseph was not a loud man, nor was he easily provoked to anger. He has always been a gentle man. That's how the boys always viewed him, but those consistent traits in Joseph didn't quash the fears that rose inside Danny, Trent, and Hayden. They all looked at the floorboard beneath them.

While still facing forward, Joseph quietly spoke to all three of them.

"Sometimes...we have extreme consequences to seemingly small wrongs we commit. It seems redundant to tell the three of you that taking something that isn't yours is wrong," he started.

"This. Today. Right now...is a scenario that you will remember for the rest of your lives. For a wrong that may seem small to you, for something that can be seen subjectively as "not a big deal," there is always an objective side to it, a factual side to it," he continued.

"A wrong is a wrong. When you decide to make the wrong decisions in your lives, no matter how big or small the wrong decision seems to you, there will always be a consequence for your actions. A wrong is a wrong no matter your perception of the situation."

"And sometimes, like today," he paused to choke back his tears, "the consequence is big."

Now all three of them were crying. Joseph put the truck in reverse and pulled out. The ride back home was quiet, and all three boys could hear their father crying while he drove back to the house.

Joseph didn't say or eat much for the next few days. After a few days passed, Danny, Trent, and Hayden came to him. He was standing outside, looking over at the pond. They asked their dad for forgiveness with solemn looks on their faces. He looked at them with glassy eyes and softly whispered, "I love you."

The boys hugged him, and their hearts were pricked the same as they were when they watched their father give up his best friend and loyal companion because of them.

Meanwhile, the Italian man and the rest of the museum crew packed up the very expensive display and all the historic relics with it. They were going to the next city listed on their calendar and staying there for a few days. They headed down the road and passed a sign that said, "Monroeville City Limits." They decided they would stop for gas at the next big city, or at least some place that had something to eat.

Forty minutes later, they pulled over to get gas and something to eat. The entire crew went inside the fast food place next to the gas station. Only one of the drivers stayed with the car and all the transport buses. He propped open the passenger side door while the gas was pumping so that he could reach his coffee. Jackson saw the open door and bolted out of the car. He ran for the street. He was fast, feeling the wind in his hair whip as he sprinted faster and faster. He ran the opposite direction they were going. Jackson was headed back to Joseph.

Once the driver realized that Jackson slipped out of the car, he ran into the fast food restaurant and shouted to the Italian man. "The dog jumped out and ran away! We need to go now and look for him!"

With a mouthful of sandwich, the man with the Italian accent said, "Don't bother. There's no telling where that dog is by now." Then he shoved a wilted piece of lettuce into his mouth.

Later that evening, Joseph was lying in bed next to his wife, thinking about Jackson and how much he loved that dog. He wondered where he was and if he felt safe. He wondered if Jackson would remember him.

Now, Jackson is a smart dog, and a loyal dog too. He made it all the way back to his own two-and-a-half-acre yard. As he trots up the driveway, he remembers the smell of the grass and trees and the big pond close by. He ran up to that same creaky, sliding, screen door and pushed on the screen in the same spot as always. Back home at last.

Going into each of the boys' rooms, he gives them a little lick on the foot or hand. When he gets to Hayden's room, Hayden hears him walk in. He sits up to look at Jackson and yells out, "Come here, buddy! I am so happy to see you! I can't believe it is you! I thought we'd never see you again!"

It had been three whole days since they left Jackson with the museum people. Hayden went running down the stairs to his parent's room, bursting in and yelling, "He's back! He's back! Jackson is back!"

Joseph and Elle both sat up straight in bed, shaken by all the yelling. Simultaneously, they both asked, "What?!"

Hayden said it again, "Jackson is back! He found his way back to us!"

This time Joseph heard what Hayden was saying and jumped out of bed to give Jackson the tightest hug ever.

Joseph cried again, and told Jackson how much he loved him and exclaimed, "I am so thankful to have you back! Thank you, God! I have missed you my best friend!"

When morning arrived, Joseph opened a can of black olives for Jackson and poured them into his bowl. Then he opened the cans of forest green and sandy beige paint colors and told the boys to come into the living room.

"We're about ready to start. Is everything covered with the tarps?"

"I don't see anything uncovered dad!" reported James.

The boys grab rollers and brushes. "We'll have this done in no time with all nine of you helping," Joseph states.

Elle peeks her head in from the kitchen and says. "It is going to look great, I just know it! This is my favorite theme for homes!" While still not understanding, little James looks at Bradly again and says, "What is mom's favorite movie? What movie theme is this?" Bradly looks at little James in a confused way.

Jackson walks over to Joseph and sits down next to his boot while he is rolling on the paint. Joseph kneels down closer to Jackson and says, "Welcome home my loyal companion. I love you very much." Jackson licks him on the nose; then Joseph stands back up to finish working on the home that he is renovating for the boys.

Part Two

THE MONOLOGUE:

Don't worry, that didn't really happen. At least as far as I know. Actually, something far greater and far worse than that happened. There was once a paradox of the worst thing and the best thing that could possibly happen in one instant. Hopefully, that story brought to life a tiny fraction of the real feelings of concern and struggle God felt at a moment much like that. It was a moment where He had to make what humans would call a "heartbreaking" decision. The moment when He decided to give us THE path back to Him, knowing it would mean trading His son for us.

We all know the story of the Gospel – how God created all mankind in His own image, and man denied Him first in the garden, then God allowed His Son to save us from eternal damnation. We can say it in our sleep. But do we really understand the struggle and tortured conflict God faced when deciding what to do about the separation we caused between ourselves and Him? Do we understand that we put Him between a rock and a hard place when we forced Him to choose between us and His only son? Even if Jesus was one of many sons, would it have been less awful to decide to give up one of your sons?

I once heard a sermon by Jay Loyd, (a preacher in Fort Smith, Arkansas) that was so inspiring to me. It helped me to better understand the love God has for us. It is a selfless love. In his sermon, he made it clear that God cannot just "do" anything. Many philosophical teachers and "higher" thinkers...or more specifically - many of the world's self-righteous individuals who choose to live a secular life, ask loaded questions like, "If God can do anything, why can't He just save everyone, regardless of their lifestyles? You claim He is God and can do anything, so why not save...everyone?" They accuse Him and say, "What? Does he just want to be mean to some people? Is this all a game?" Or they smirk while backing you into a corner by asking hypothetical questions like, "If God can do anything, can He make a rock that is too big for Himself to lift?" They become proud when you start to get uncomfortable.

The simple answer to their rhetorical questions is "No." God cannot do anything. It sounds uncomfortable for us to say because we have been told since we were old enough to comprehend sentences that "God can do anything!" However, that is simply a false narrative made up by men and women alike. We use it to put the blame on God if someone dies - (Well, God could do anything, and He let that innocent person die!) Or maybe we use it to speak about our own prosperity - (God can do anything! I believe He will make me happy and wealthy!) Sounds like typical human babbling.

To be clear...

God cannot deny Himself. God is righteous. God is truthful. God is Just. God is perfect. If God were to accept sin (man was sin since we chose to be sinful), then He would be denying His own perfectness. If He were to choose sin, even though He does not sin, He would be choosing unrighteousness, even though He is righteous. If He were to make a rock that is too big for Himself to lift, is that not the epitome of denying Himself? The Bible states that He cannot deny Himself and He cannot lie. (2 Timothy 2:13 and Hebrews 6:18)

God is bound by His own righteousness, truthfulness,

perfectness, and justness. If He exceeds those bounds, then He is not God. So, no--- God cannot just do anything. For the sake of not sounding like these words belittle God, let me be more clear. God can do anything that is within His will. His will is to be purely righteous, perfect, just, and truthful. For the things that are within the bounds of God's will and His greatness, He can do anything. We pervert this simple concept when we make it our will and not God's will. Thus, we have mass confusion rooted in selfishness and personal gain.

To help you visualize how and why God cannot do anything, consider these words I heard my husband say once when explaining the justness of God: "We have the greatest country in the world and it's in part due to how our judicial system is set up. Each judge that takes the oath and sits on the bench is expected by the people to uphold the law. Imagine a judge has a daughter and that daughter chooses to do something wrong, illegal in fact! Imagine she ends up in her father's courtroom. He is a noble judge who is thoughtful about each case that comes before him and always applies the United States' laws to each case in an unbiased fashion. Visualize his daughter standing before him in court and everyone knowing she is guilty and he as the judge dismisses her wrongs as if they never happened. He does not hold her accountable the same as he does everyone else that comes through his courtroom. Well, the people of this great country wouldn't stand for that! That isn't right, just because that is his daughter. If he did that, then he wouldn't be an honest judge bound by the laws of this land. He would be denying the very oath he took. The same scenario applies to God. Just as all of our judges cannot just do anything and still be judges, God cannot just do anything and still be God. Judges are bound by the law and justice and God is bound by His righteousness. We certainly hope He is a just God and not making up the rules as He goes. He is bound by His own righteousness and perfectness. If He goes outside those bounds, then He is not God."

The "behind the scenes" story to the Gospel is the story of the torturing conflict God faced when deciding to allow or not allow His only son to pay the redeeming price (becoming full of sin and dying for it) to let us have a way to live in heaven, when we were the ones who chose to deny God and His Son and separate ourselves from them in the first place. What a mouth full! The mental anguish and conflict God felt when looking at us and knowing how much He loved us, His creation, and then turning to look at His loyal companion and son and determining which He would be less emotional about leaving behind is unimaginable. How vulnerable humans were at that moment when He was conflicted. Does He choose these creatures walking on Earth, who have already denied Him in the beginning weeks of their existence? Or does He choose His son who has been with Him forever and who is innocent of any wrongdoing? There was one verdict for us, just like the daughter in her father's courtroom. Guilty. We would either go down for it, or Jesus would. He was the only one pure enough to take on the weight of sin and give us salvation. That is why it had to be Him for us, if there was going to be a path to heaven at all.

The sadness and struggling concern He must have felt

while being bound by His own righteousness to have simply one choice to make - if He were to choose to save us, must have been nauseating. It had to be a trade for trade. Innocent for the guilty. A break even. Jesus was the only one who could pay the price tag hanging around our necks. He was the currency that bought out the sin and did away with it. Only then did sin take Him with it, while He became it. You see, it wasn't a simple list: <u>choice 1 for salvation</u>, <u>choice 2 for salvation</u>, <u>choice 3 for salvation</u> or <u>choice 4, send your innocent son to die for these creatures' sins</u>. **There was one choice. It was Jesus for us or nothing for us. We would either have the way back to Him through Jesus, or we would have nothing, and be rightfully condemned for eternity.**

How humbling. It is amazing that God actually loved us that much. And Jesus shares the same selfless love for us as His father does. He willingly did it, and nothing was forced on Him. There are no words, other than, *"...that's not what I would have done had it been me determining between my sweet son, Nathan, and the selfish people of this world."* To be honest, in reference to the story, I don't think I would even give up my dogs for the selfish people of the world. Of course, that is my initial human thought.

Consider taking your mind here: In the story, even though there was a strong emotional attachment to the dog, to any person in that situation, the choice would still be very clear. The decision is really no decision. The person would give up the dog because the sons are of greater value than a dog, even a special dog. In God's decision, it would have been the other way around---giving up His son for a dog. To rewrite the story illustrating Joseph giving up His son to save the dog, would offend us. No one would relate to that because no one would believe someone would actually give up their son for the sake of their dog. *I can't write a story like that!* No one would read it, and they certainly wouldn't read it to their children before bedtime. We don't want to read stories like that because it is not relatable. It is unspeakable to give up a son for a dog---yet that is what God did. In the story, the lesser was given for the greater. In God's case, the greater was given for the lesser. That thought alone, is why so many Christians struggle with fully comprehending what God really did for us. Hopefully, the fictional story is relatable to us, so that we may understand a small fraction of the struggle God faced in that decision. But even our greatest comprehension of God's sacrifice is next to nothing in terms of fully understanding what was done when He gave up His Son for a dog.

The story of the man with his dog is fictional, but it has a greater meaning for driving an emotional connection with God. **It is necessary to have an emotional connection to God.** Our service to Him is more than a rigid "to do" list of commandments. We have an emotional relationship with Him. Our human nature pushes us to cling to emotional things in our lives.

Consider things or people that you have formed emotional bonds with: a song, a TV character, parents, family members, friends, and the list goes on and on. These things and people mean a lot to us because we have an emotional connection to them.

It is our human responsibility to form an emotional bond with God. It is your duty, if you want God to have an emotional place in your heart. In order for God to take His rightful place in your life, you need an emotional connection with Him. Like Paul said "...work out your own salvation..." (Philippians 2:12). The message is clear, a big part of salvation will be forming an emotional connection with God.

In your moments of quiet, think about this story. The father, his dog, and his sons. It provokes the reader to examine his or her relationship with God, especially with forming a loyal and emotional connection with God. For everything that has ever been done for you, even the altruistic things – as rare as they may be on Earth, the greatest thing that was ever done for you was God trading His son to buy out your sins and give you an eternal life with Him.

It is hard to believe that God made that decision in our favor, but He did. Thank You God for your son, Jesus. It is glorious to know that I will see Your greatness one day. We are forever indebted to you.

Part Three

THE STUDY GUIDE:

By a certain age, we are more loyal to and likely to live by what is right when we come to the conclusions on our own. In this section, my hope is that the questions are discussed using the Socratic method. That is, by asking open-ended, follow-up questions and moving the discussions along, with everyone engaged. When analyzing these questions with the younger people in your lives, consider guiding their thinking instead of telling them the answers. By doing this, it will allow them to understand how they can relate to the story and reach their own conclusions about how great God is. It will be their thoughts with your guidance. They will own it and take more pride in their relationship with God, as well as become loyal followers. This transformation in understanding what God has done happens when they arrive at the answers on their own.

It is best to re-evaluate yourself often. It is also best to be honest in this section. Being honest with yourself and with God will help you obtain a closeness to Him you have not yet grasped.

QUESTIONS:

1) From this list, circle all the phrases that most accurately describe your current relationship with God. Remember to circle all that apply:
   A) like a pal for the good times
   B) like an acquaintance you hardly know
   C) strictly business
   D) someone you fear
   E) someone you love
   F) like a distant relative you see for the holidays
   G) like a Supreme Court Justice upholding the law
   H) like a police officer enforcing the law
   I) like a friend to confide in
   J) like a big brother always watching you
   K) like a scary boss breathing down your neck
   L) like your psychiatrist for emotional problems
   M) something else

2) In your own words, briefly describe your relationship with God.

3) Briefly explain what goes on in your life that keeps God in the relationship status He is currently in with you.

4) List two things that you do not think fondly of: (for example---an itchy sweater or a clingy cat)

5) List two things that you do think fondly of: (for example---ice cream or warm breeze)

6) What kinds of adjectives (words to describe) do you use when referencing the things you do not think fondly of: (for example---ugly, annoying)

7) What kinds of adjectives (words to describe) do you use when referencing the things you do think fondly of: (for example---delicious, exciting)

8) What kinds of adjectives (words to describe) do you use when referencing God:

9) Do you believe that word-association and the way you speak or think about things is a way of training your mind to think about something or someone a certain way? (For example, always referring to your neighbor as an annoying person will inherently train your mind to dislike that person.) Do you believe this is true? Yes or No?

10) What kind of word-association, speech, or thought do you use when thinking of or referring to God?

11) Look at the words you just listed. Do they reinforce good or bad feelings about God?

12) Describe your interaction with God on a daily, weekly, or monthly basis.

13) Do you feel your relationship with God could be better than it is?

14) What are you doing to make that happen?

15) How often do you think about God trading His Son for you?

16) How often are you asked, or how often do you ask yourself hypothetical questions like, "Why can't or why won't God just save everyone?"

17) Do you feel you have an answer for that question? If so, briefly explain.

18) In a paragraph, describe *why* you think you should strive to grasp the unimaginable pain God went through for you. Explain why doing so is important in developing your healthy relationship with Him.

ANSWERS/OPINIONS:

1-2) It is likely you circled and listed more than one type of relationship description. **That's okay!** Most people feel they have a complex relationship with God that can't be described with just one word or phrase. ~**Isaiah 41:10**~

3) In most cases, people don't just place God in a certain type of relationship role and decide that is where He is going to stay. He is usually placed there based on what is going on in your life or not going on in your life. If you are neglecting your relationship with God, it is safe to say He will be placed in the role of "acquaintance." If you are going through the loss of a loved one, He may be placed in the role of "psychiatrist or counselor." The things that happen or don't happen in our lives put a lot of emphasis on our relationship with God. Some things in life are uncontrollable, but many things are. It is your responsibility to take every situation in your life, good and bad, and nurture it to help your relationship with God. **There is no such thing as being in neutral.** You are constantly either moving closer to Him or further from Him. You are the pilot of that plane. ~**2 Timothy 2:15 / Matthew 7:16-20 / 1 Thessalonians 5:16-18 / Philippians 4:6-7**~

4-11) You are what you eat and things *are what you think!* I don't mean that your perception of something can never be wrong, I mean the way you think about things is the way they will be to you---regardless of whether you are right or wrong about them. Like the example listed earlier---(you referring to your neighbor as always being annoying gives you little to no room in your mind to give them any good qualities). You can't do that---you would be contradicting yourself! So, to justify your thoughts, you stay on that path when referring to that person---"They aren't only annoying, they are also rude and overflow their trash-cans!" You are training yourself in the way you will perceive them. You can easily do the same thing with God. It is easier for us to stay on one path of thinking than it is to cross over back and forth. It feels inconsistent to us. And for fear of being called out on our inconsistencies, we decide it is safer to stay on the chosen route when referring to someone or something. Your definition, word-association, thought, and talk about God is critical to your relationship with Him. You either think positively or negatively about Him. You may even think of God or religion as annoying. It will all depend on how you train your mind to think about God. That is in your control. What is not in your control, is God's greatness. God is God. Your adjectives and definition of Him will not change Him, it will only change your thinking (for better or worse) about Him. **~Romans 12:2 / Philippians 2:5 / Philippians 4:8 / Proverbs 23:7~**

12) The amount of time you spend interacting with God is a direct correlation to what kind of relationship you will have with Him. It is as simple as that. The amount of effort you put in will either help you or hurt you. **Put in the right effort! ~Matthew 6:6 / Psalm 145: 18-19~**

13-14) I hope you feel your relationship could use some improvement. Most things can always be improved, especially your relationship with God. It is the most important thing of all! Once you have made a list of things you think you should do to help your relationship with God grow---Do them! **Yes, usually "it is the thought that counts." But not in this case.** You need to do it. ~**James 1:22 / James 2:18**~

15) This is the **foundation of your faith.** Bring it into your thought process as often as you can. It is the only reason you can have **real happiness** in your life. ~**Romans 15:13 / 1 Peter 1:8-9 / 1 Peter 3:18 / 1 Corinthians 2:9 / 2 Corinthians 5:15 / John 3:16 / Psalm 47:1**~

16-17) It is human nature to ask these types of questions and you will likely hear them at some point in your life. But if you are being honest when asking and not trying to find a reason to turn from God, you will see the answer is very simple and clear. He is a just God and cannot do everything. Trust me, you wouldn't want a God who isn't just. That would be scary for everyone. **Try finding *peace* in a God who you can't trust! It won't be easy!** We can have peace in His faithfulness and justness. He is pure truth, just, righteous, and cannot deny Himself. Because He is just, He cannot accept sin. If He did, He would be denying His own righteousness and He would not be God. God is bound by His own righteousness and truthfulness. Again, we don't want Him to step outside His bounds of righteousness because if He did, He wouldn't be a just God. Every promise He made to us and the peace He offers to us would be gone - out the window. For God to be God---all powerful and just, He must be a God who does not deny Himself. God will not deny Himself. Will you deny Him? **~Colossians 2:8 / Philippians 4:7 / Titus 1:2 / 2 Timothy 2:13 / 2 Timothy 2:16~**

18) Just like the answer to number 15, this speaks to the foundation of your faith. Push yourself to reach a better understanding of what God went through when He sacrificed His Son for you. As for the reason for *why* you should do such a thing- doing so will make it more of a reality to you instead of just a story that happened a long time ago. **It will pull out of you your natural human emotions** and help you have a greater desire to be close to God. That is why you should strive to understand the mental conflict God went through at that moment when He traded His Son for you. Choose to live for Jesus and keep His commandments. **~John 17:20-23 / Matthew 27:46 / Romans 8:32 / 1 John 4:9 / 2 Peter 1:17~**

Once we have a better understanding of what God really did for us when He made the decision to save us, we can have a better love for Him, a better respect for Him, a better relationship with Him, and a greater desire to be with Him and His Son in Heaven, when the time comes.

Inspired by one of the best sermons I have ever heard. This sermon, "God Cannot Do Anything" by Jay Loyd, helped me to better understand the real love of God and the mental conflict He faced when choosing to give us the path back to Him. He was justified to turn from us forever, and He sadly and lovingly decided to do the deal---a trade for trade---the innocent for the guilty, which was the only choice, aside from leaving us forever. He could have let us go forever and be justified, or let the innocent Jesus go. Either let the boys go and be justified in doing so, or let the innocent, loyal companion go. What a mentally conflicting place we put God in by our first denial of Him and His greatness. Thank you, Jay, for your continued thoughtful study and insightful sermons.

www.ingramcontent.com/pod-product-compliance
Lightning Source LLC
Chambersburg PA
CBHW050608300426
44112CB00013B/2123